BOOKS BY **ROBERT E. DALEY**

A Case for "Threes"
A Simple Plan . . . of Immense Complexity
Armour, Weapons, And Warfare
from Everlasting to Everlasting
Killer Sex
Life or Death, Heaven or Hell, You Choose!
Raptures and Resurrections
Short Tales
So . . . What Happens to the Package?
Study and Interpretation of The Scriptures Made Simple
Surviving Destruction as A Human Being
The Gospel of John
The Gospel of John (Red Edition)
The League of The Immortals
The New Testament - Pauline Revelation
The New Testament - Pauline Revelation Companion
"The World That Then Was . . ." & The Genesis That Now Is
What Color Are You?
What Makes A Christian Flaky?
What Really Happened to Judas Iscariot?
Who YOU Are in Christ . . . RIGHT NOW!

The Enhancement Series

#2 Book of Daniel
#3 Book of Romans
#4 Book of Galatians
#5 Book of Hebrews

The Deeper Things of God Series

#1 The Personage of God
#2 The Personage of Man
#3 The Personage of Christ

The Enhancement Series • Book One

THE OLD TESTAMENT

BOOK OF ECCLESIASTES

OR, THE PREACHER

ENHANCED

Enjoy the Book of Ecclesiastes
as set forth in understandable
language through original
King James Translation
with *Enhancement*

Robert E. Daley

The Larry Czerwonka Company, LLC
Hilo, Hawai'i

First Edition — November 2014

This book is set in 14-point Garamond

Published by: The Larry Czerwonka Company, LLChttp://thelarryczerwonkacompany.com

Printed in the United States of America

ISBN:0692330097
ISBN-13:978-0692330098

All scriptures used in this work are taken from the King James Version of the Scriptures.

Introduction

The Book of Ecclesiastes is a work that is attributed to King Solomon, while he was in a spiritually backslidden condition. The work is additionally known of by many as *The Preacher*. The theme of the book is the futility of Man trying to be happy apart from having a relationship with the living God. The main focus word within the whole of the book is *vanity*.

King Solomon was the wisest, richest, most influential king that the Nation of Israel had ever had. His perspective of viewing things *under the sun* finds life in this world to be empty despite a person having power, prestige, popularity, pleasure, or any other chattel possessions.

Within each Human-Being, by a divine design, there is a *God-shaped* vacuum that is awaiting the filling-up-of, by the One and only Holy Spirit of God. Without that vacuum being correctly filled with the Spirit of God himself, attempts will be made to fill it with drugs, sex, money, influence, and many other worldly substitutes, that men pursue vigorously, and at great expense, but that ultimately render no genuine peace or satisfaction. "Vanity, vanity, all is vanity" *(Ecclesiastes 12:8)*.

The enhancement that is provided within this work will hopefully not only bring clarity, but provide possibly a fresh perspective to the spiritual realities that are touched upon by King Solomon.

Our prayer is that you will enjoy the presentation, and share this small work with others.

THE BOOK OF
ECCLESIASTES

CHAPTER 1

1.   The words of *Solomon* the Preacher, the son of David *the* king, *as he abode* in Jerusalem.

2.   Vanity of vanities, saith *Solomon* the Preacher, vanity of vanities; all *is certainly* vanity.

3.   What *eternal* profit hath a *sinful* man of all *of* his labor which he *hath* taketh under the sun?

4.   *One* generation passeth away *and is gone*, and *another* generation cometh *in its place*. But the earth *continues to* abideth for ever*more, without even taking notice.*

5.   The sun also ariseth *early*, and *then* the sun goeth down, and hasteth *back again* to his place where he *first* arose.

6.   The wind goeth toward the south, and *then* turneth about *and goeth* unto the north. It whirleth about continually, and the wind returneth again *and again* according to his circuits.

7.   All *of* the rivers *eventually* run into the sea, yet the sea *is* not *ever* full. Unto the *same* place, from whence the rivers *originally* come, thither they return again.

8.   All things *on the earth* **are** full of labor; *and yet sinful* man cannot utter *the fullness of* **it.** The eye *of sinful man* is not satisfied with *the* seeing, nor the ear *ever* filled with *the* hearing.

9.   The thing that hath *already* been, it *is that* which shall *come to* be *again.* And that which is *already* done *is* that which shall *come to* be done *again.* And, *there is* no new *thing* under the sun.

10.   Is there *any* thing whereof it may be said, See *this*, this *is* new *isn't it?* It hath been already of *an* old time, which was before us.

11.   *There is usually* no remembrance of former *things, which is why history repeats itself;* neither shall there be *any* remembrance of *things* that are to come with *those people* that shall come after, *because sinful people are still people, and sinful people will still do what sinful people continue to do.*

12.   I *Solomon* the Preacher was *the* king over *the Nation of* Israel, *and I abode* in Jerusalem.

13.   And I gave my heart to seek and *to* search out, by *using natural* wisdom, concerning all *of the things* that are *now* done under *the* heaven. This sore travail *of searching* hath God given *un*to the sons of *sinful* man to be exercised therewith.

14.   I have seen all *of* the works *of sinful man* that are done under the sun. And, behold, all *of it is a* vanity and *a* vexation of *the* spirit.

15. *That which is* crooked cannot *easily* be made straight. And that which is *sore* wanting cannot be *accurately* numbered.

16. I communed with mine own heart, saying, Lo, I am come to *the place of having a* great estate, and have gotten more *natural* wisdom *from God* than all *they* that have been *on the throne* before me in Jerusalem. Yea, my heart had great experience of *both natural* wisdom and *increased* knowledge.

17. And I gave my heart to know *natural* wisdom, and to know *about both* madness and folly. *And* I perceived that this also is *a* vexation of *the* spirit.

18. For in much *natural* wisdom *there is also* much grief. And he that increaseth *in* knowledge, increaseth *also in* sorrow.

CHAPTER 2

1. I said in mine heart, Go to now, I will prove thee *O heart* with mirth, therefore enjoy *thy* pleasure. And, behold, this also *is proven to be* vanity.

2. I said of laughter, *It is* mad. And of mirth, What doeth it, *and what good is it?*

3. I sought in mine heart to give myself unto *excess of* wine, *while* yet acquainting mine heart with *natural* wisdom *at the same time.* And to lay hold on folly, *un*til I might see what *it was* that *was going to be* good for the sons of men, which they should *put their hand forth to* do under the heaven, all *of* the days of their life.

4.   I made me great works. I builded me *multiple* houses. I planted me *extensive* vineyards.

5.   I made me *fabulous* gardens and *plenteous* orchards, and I planted *various* trees in them, of all **kind of** fruits.

6.   I made me pools of water, to water therewith the wood*ed area,* that bringeth forth *the various kinds of* trees.

7.   I got *me multiple* servants and maidens, and had *many* servants born in my *own* house. Also, I had great possessions of great and small cattle above all that were in Jerusalem before me.

8.   I gathered me *together* also silver and gold, and the peculiar treasure of kings, and *the wealth* of the provinces. I gat me *numerous* men singers, and *numerous* women singers, and *such as were* the delights of the sons of men, *like as of* musical instruments, and that of all *different* sorts.

9.   So I was *truly* great, and increased more than all that were *kings* before me in Jerusalem; also, my *natural* wisdom *still* remained with me.

10.   And whatsoever mine eyes desired *to see,* I kept not from them. I withheld not my heart from

any joy *that it desired.* For my heart rejoiced in all *of* my labor. And this *delight* was my *allotted* portion of all *of* my labor.

11.   Then I looked *up*on all *of* the works that my hands had wrought, and on *all of* the labour that I had laboured to do. And, behold, all *of it* **was** vanity and vexation of *the* spirit, and ***there was*** no *spiritual* profit *in it* under the sun.

12.   And I turned myself to behold *my own natural* wisdom, and *it was* madness, and folly. For what **can** *even* the *common* man*, or the new king* **do,** that cometh after the *current* king? ***Even*** *only* that, which hath been already done *before.*

13.   Then I saw that *natural* wisdom *without spiritual influence,* excelleth *in* folly, as far as *the* light excelleth *against the* darkness.

14.   The wise *sinful* man's eyes *are* in his head, but the fool walketh in *abject* darkness. And I myself perceived also, that one event happeneth *equally* to them all.

15.   Then said I in my heart, As it happeneth to the fool, so it happeneth even to me: and why was I then more wise? Then I said in my heart, that this also *is* vanity.

16.   For ***there is*** no remembrance of the wise *man* more than of the fool*ish man* for ever. Seeing *that* that which now *is,* in the days to come, shall

all be forgotten. And how dieth the wise *man any differently, than* as the fool?

17.   Therefore I hated *this* life. Because *all of* the work that is wrought under the sun, *is* grievous unto me. For all *of it is* vanity and vexation of *the* spirit.

18.   Yea, I hated all *of* my labour which I had taken under the sun. Because I should leave it *in the end, even* unto the man that shall be after me.

19.   And who *is to* knoweth whether *or not* he shall be a wise *man* or a fool? Yet, *either way,* shall he have rule over all *of* my labour wherein I have laboured, and wherein I have shewed myself *to be* wise under the sun. This also is *a* vanity.

20.   Therefore I went about to cause my heart to despair of all *of* the labour which I took *to do* under the sun.

21.   For there is a man whose labour *is* in *natural* wisdom, and in *increased* knowledge, and in *true* equity. Yet to a man that hath not *even* laboured therein, shall he leave it *for* his portion. This also *is a* vanity and a great evil.

22.   For *in the end,* what hath *that sinful* man of all *of* his labour, and of the vexation of his heart, wherein he hath laboured *his whole life* under the sun?

23.	For all *of* his days *are the days of* sorrows, and his travail *truly* grief. Yea, his heart taketh not *any* rest in the night. This is also *a* vanity.

24.	*There is* nothing better for a *sinful* man, *than* that he should eat and drink, and *that* he should make his soul enjoy *the* good *that is* in his labour. This also I saw, that it *was* from the hand of *the* *Lord my* God.

25.	For who can eat, or who else can hasten *hereunto, any* more than I?

26.	For *God* giveth to a *righteous* man that *which is* good in his sight, *natural* wisdom, and *increased* knowledge, and *true* joy. But to the sinner he giveth *only to* travail, *and* to gather and to heap up *goods, so* that he may give *it* to *him that is righteous and* good before God. This also *is a* vanity and vexation of *the* spirit.

CHAPTER 3

1.	To every *thing that occurs* *there is* a season, and a time to every purpose under the heaven.

2.	A time to be born, and a time to die. A time to plant and a time to pluck up *that which is* planted.

3.	A time to kill, and a time to heal. A time to break down, and a time to build up.

4.   A time to weep, and a time to laugh. A time to mourn, and a time to dance.

5.   A time to cast away stones, and a time to gather stones together. A time to embrace, and a time to refrain from embracing.

6.   A time to get, and a time to lose. A time to keep, and a time to cast away.

7.   A time to rend, and a time to sew. A time to keep silence, and a time to speak.

8.   A time to love, and a time to hate. A time of war, and a time of peace.

9.   What *eternal* profit hath he that worketh, in that wherein he *applieth himself to* laboureth?

10.   I have seen the travail *of life*, which God hath given to the sons of *sinful* men to be exercised in it.

11.   He hath made every *thing* beautiful in his time. Also, he hath set the world in their heart *because of sin*, so that no man can find out the work *of redemption* that God maketh from the beginning to the end *of the probation*.

12.   I know that *there is really* no good in them, but for *a sinful* **man** to *temporarily* rejoice, and *then* to do *whatever* good *that he can,* in his life.

13.   And also that every man should eat and drink, and enjoy the good of all *of* his labour, *for* it *is* the gift of God.

14. I know that, whatsoever God doeth *concerning redemption*, it shall be *something that shall last* for ever. Nothing can be put to it *to improve on it*, nor any thing *done that can be* taken *away* from it. And God *alone* doeth *it*, that *men* should *walk in godly* fear before him.

15. That which hath *already* been, *and* is *manifest even* now, and that which is to be *in the future,* hath already been *in days gone by.* And God requireth *accountability concerning* that which is past.

16. And moreover, I saw under the sun the place of judgment, *that* wickedness *was resident* there. And the place of righteousness, *that* iniquity *was even* there *also.*

17. I said in mine heart, God shall judge *both* the righteous and the wicked. For *there is* a time *scheduled* there, for every purpose and for every work.

18. I said in mine heart concerning the *sinful* estate of the sons of men, that God might *make* manifest *unto* them *the truth.* And that they might *be able to* see, that they themselves are *no better off than the* beasts *of the field.*

19. For that *heinous condition,* which befalleth the sons of men, *also* befalleth *the* beasts *of the field.* Even one thing befalleth them *all.* As the one dieth, so dieth the other. Yea, they have all *only* one breath. So that a *sinful* man hath no preeminence above *that of* a beast. For all *is a* vanity.

20.   All *sinful men* go unto *the* one place. All *sinful men* are of the dust *of the ground*, and all *shall re*turn to *the* dust again.

21.   Who knoweth *of* the spirit of *a* man that *eventually* goeth upward, and the spirit of the beast that goeth downward *in*to the earth?

22.   Wherefore I perceive that *there is currently* nothing better, than that a man should rejoice in his own works *on this earth*. For that *is* allotted *as* his portion. For who shall *be able to* bring him to see what shall be after him?

CHAPTER 4

1.   So I returned *unto my chamber*, and considered all *of* the oppressions that are done under the sun. And behold, *I considered* the tears of *such as were* oppressed, and *that* they had no comforter. And on the side of their oppressors there was *demonstrated* power, but they had no comforter.

2.   Wherefore I praised the dead, which are already dead *and out of their miseries*, more than the living which are yet alive *and still suffering*.

3.   Yes, better *is he* than both, they which hath not yet been, *and also they* who hath not *as yet* seen the evil work that is done under the sun.

4.   Again, I considered all *of the* travail *that I have seen*, and every right work *as well*, that for this a man is envied of his neighbor. This *is* also *a* vanity and vexation of *the* spirit.

5.   The fool foldeth his hands together, and eateth his own flesh.

6.   Better *is just* an handful *with* quietness, than both the hands full *with* travail and vexation of *the* spirit.

7.   Then I returned *again*, and I saw *more* vanity under the sun.

8.   There is one *man* **alone**, and *there is* not a second *man with him*. Yea, he hath neither child nor brother *to help him*, yet *is there* no end of all *of* his labour. Neither is his eye satisfied with riches *that he might attain*. Neither **saith he,** For whom do I labour, and bereave my soul of goods? This *is* also *a* vanity, yea, it *is* a sore travail.

9.   Two *are* better than one, because they *are able to assist one another, and* have a good reward for their labour.

10.   For if they fall, the one will *be able to* lift up his fellow. But woe *un*to him *that is all* alone when

he falleth, for *he hath* not another *one* to help him *get* up *again*.

11.   Again, if two *individuals* lie *down* together, then they have heat *between them*, but how can one *person* be warm *when he is all* **alone**?

12.   And if one *shall* prevail **against him,** *then* two shall *be able to* withstand him. And a threefold cord is not quickly broken.

13.   Better *is* a poor and a wise child than an old and foolish king, who will no more *allow himself to* be admonished.

14.   For out of *a* prison he cometh to reign. Whereas also *he that is* born in his kingdom becometh poor *because of the character of the king*.

15.   I considered all *of* the living *people* which walk under the sun, with the second child that shall *come along and* stand up in his stead.

16.   *There is* no end of all *of* the people, *even* of all that have been before them. They also that come after shall not rejoice in him. Surely this also *is a* vanity and vexation of *the* spirit.

CHAPTER 5

1.   Keep thy foot when thou goest *in*to the house of God, and be more ready to hear *the instruction of the word of the Lord,* than to give the *carnal*

sacrifice of fools. For they consider not *the spiritual reality* that they do evil.

2.   Be not *foolish and* rash with thy mouth, and let not thine heart be hasty to utter *any* thing *unwise* before God. For God *is* *dwelling* in heaven, and thou *art* upon *the* earth. Therefore let thy words be few, *and carefully chosen.*

3.   For a*n* *unconscious* dream cometh *about* through the multitude of *conscious* business. And a fool's voice is *truly* **known** by *the* multitude of *the* words *that cometh forth from him.*

4.   When thou vowest a vow, *and commit thyself* unto God, defer not to pay it. For *he hath* no pleasure in fools *that consider not the word that they have spoken.* Pay that which thou hast vowed.

5.   Better *is it* that thou *shouldest* not vow, than that thou shouldest *go ahead and* vow, and *then* not pay.

6.   Suffer not thy mouth to cause *the rest of* thy flesh to sin. Neither say thou before the angel, that it *was* an error, *and I really did not mean it.* Wherefore should God be angry at thy voice, and *shall* destroy the work of thine hands?

7.   For in the multitude of dreams and *of* many words, *there are* also *divers* vanities. But *be wise, and chooseth to* fear thou God.

8.   If thou seest the oppression of the poor, and *the* violent perverting of judgment and justice in a province, marvel not at the matter. For *he that is* higher than the highest *also seeth, and* regardeth. And *there be even* higher than they.

9.   Moveover the profit of the *provision of the* earth is for all. The king *himself* is served by the field.

10.   He that loveth silver shall not be *ultimately* satisfied with silver, *he shall want more*. Nor *shall* he that loveth abundance *be satisfied* with increase. This *is* also *a* vanity.

11.   When *earthly* goods *do* increase, they *also* are increased that *do* eat them. And what good *is there perchance* to the owners thereof, saving *for* the beholding *of them* with their eyes?

12.   The sleep of a labouring man *is* sweet, *despite* whether he eat*eth even very* little or much. But the abundance of the rich will not suffer him to sleep *soundly, because of the fear of loss*.

13.   There is a sore evil *which* I have seen under the sun, *namely,* riches *held onto and* kept for the owners thereof *even* to their *own* hurt.

14.   But those riches perish *as well* by evil travail. And he begetteth a son, and *behold,* *there is* nothing *with*in his hand.

15.   As he came forth of his mother's womb, naked shall he return to go as he came, and shall

take nothing of his labour which he may carry away in his hand.

16.   And this also is a sore evil, *that* in all points as he came *in naked*, so shall he go *out naked*. And what profit hath he *to enjoy? Only* that *he* hath laboured for the wind.

17.   All *of* his days also, he eateth in *the* darkness. And *he hath* much sorrow and wrath *to go along* with his sickness.

18.   Behold *that* which I have seen: *it is* good and comely *for one* to eat and to drink, and to enjoy the good of all *of* his labour that he taketh under the sun all *of* the days of his life, which God giveth *unto* him. For it *is* his portion.

19.   Every man also to whom God hath *graciously* given riches and wealth, and hath given him power to eat *of the fruit* thereof, and to take his portion, and to rejoice in *all of* his labour; this *is* the gift of God.

20.   For *when the time cometh,* he shall not much remember the *adverse* days of his life; because God answereth *him within* the *inner man, in the* joy of his heart.

CHAPTER 6

1.   There is an evil which I have *personally* seen under the sun, and it *is* *something that is* common among men.

2.   A man to whom God hath given riches, wealth, and honour, so that he wanteth *for* nothing for his soul, of all that he desireth; yet God giveth him not *the* power to eat *of it* thereof, but a stranger *doth* eateth it. This *is* *a* vanity, and it *is* an evil disease.

3.   If a man beget an hundred *children*, and live many years, so that the days of his years be many, and his soul be not filled with good, and also *that* *in the end* he have no burial; I say, *that* an untimely birth *is* better *off* than he.

4.   For he cometh in*to* *this world* with vanity, and departeth in *spiritual* darkness, and his name shall be *forever* covered with darkness.

5.   Moreover he hath not seen the sun, nor known *any thing:* this *one* hath more rest than the other.

6.   Yea, though he live a thousand years twice *told*, yet hath he seen no good. Do not all *individuals* *ultimately* go in*to* one place, *before the resurrection of Christ?*

7.   All the labour of *sinful* man *is* for *the benefit of* his mouth, and yet the appetite is not *ever* filled.

8.   For what *advantage* hath the wise *sinful man* more than the *sinful* fool? What *advantage* hath the poor *sinful man*, that knoweth *how* to walk before the living?

9.   Better *is* the sight of the eyes than the wandering of the desire. This *is* also *a* vanity and *a* vexation of *the* spirit.

10.   That which hath been *in the past* is named already, and it is *well* known that it *is of sinful* man. Neither may he *successfully* contend with him that is mightier than he.

11.   Seeing there be many things that increase vanity, *ultimately* what *is sinful* man the better *for it all?*

12.   For who knoweth what *is* good for *any sinful* man in *this* life, all *of* the days of his vain life which he spendeth *are* as a shadow? For who can tell *unto* a *sinful* man what shall be after him, under the sun.

CHAPTER 7

1.   *To establish* a good name *is much* better than precious ointment. And the day of *one's* death *is better* than the day of one's birth, *if he is redeemed.*

2. *It is* better to go *in*to the house of mourning *for reflection*, than to go *in*to the house of feasting *and lust*. For that *is* the *undoing and the* end of all *sinful* men, and the living *man who is wise* will lay *it* to his heart.

3. Sorrow *is* better than laughter. For by the sadness of the countenance the *very* heart is made better.

4. The heart of the wise *is repentant, and* in the house of mourning, but the heart of fools *is* in the house of mirth.

5. *It is* better to hear the rebuke of the wise, than for a man to hear the *foolish* song*s* of fools.

6. For as the crackling of thorns *burning* under a pot, so *is* the *hollow* laughter of the fool. This also *is a* vanity.

7. Surely oppression *can tend to* maketh a wise man mad. And a gift *of bribery* destroyeth the heart.

8. Better *is* the end of a thing than the beginning thereof. *And* the patient in spirit *is much* better *off* than the proud in spirit.

9. Be not hasty *with*in thy spirit to be angry. For anger resteth in the bosom of fools.

10. Say not thou, What is *the cause* that the former days were better than these? For thou dost not enquire wisely concerning this *in looking toward the past*.

11. *Natural* wisdom *is* good *along* with an inheritance. And *by it, there is* *potential* **profit,** to them that see the sun.

12. For *natural* wisdom *is* a defense *against the ravages of life,* *and* money *is* a defense *against financial devastation.* But the excellency of knowledge *is, that* *godly* wisdom giveth *eternal* life, to them that have it.

13. Consider the work of God. For who *else* can make *that* straight, which he hath *originally* made crooked?

14. In the day of prosperity be joyful, but in the day of adversity consider *what you have believed and have done.* God also hath set the one over against the other, to the end that man should *consider his life,* *and* find nothing after him.

15. All *things* have I seen in the days of my vanity. There is a just *man* that perisheth *even* in his righteousness, and there is a wicked *man* that prolongeth *his life* *even with*in his wickedness.

16. Be not righteous over much, *depending upon* *your own goodness, and not God's grace, to save you.* Neither make thyself over wise, *in leaning unto thine own understanding. For* why shouldest thou *aggravate thy sinfulness,* *and* destroy thyself *before thy time* ?

17 Be not over much wicked, neither be thou foolish. *For* why shouldest thou die before thy time?

18.   *It is a* good *thing* that thou shouldest take hold of this *that I am telling you.* Yea, also from this withdraw not thine hand. For he that feareth God shall *emerge, and* come forth of them all.

19.   *Natural* wisdom strentheneth the wise man more that ten mighty *men* which are *with*in the city.

20.   For *there is* not a just man upon the earth, that doeth good and sinneth not.

21.   Also take no heed unto all *of the* words that are spoken, lest thou hear thy servant curse thee.

22.   For oftentimes also thine own heart knoweth that thou thyself likewise hast cursed others.

23.   All *of* this have I proved by *natural* wisdom. I said, I will *purpose to* be wise. But it *was* far from me.

24.   That which is far off, and exceeding*ly* deep, who can find it out?

25.   I applied mine heart to know, and to search, and to seek out *natural* wisdom, and the reason *of things,* and to know the wickedness of folly, even *to know* of foolishness *and* madness.

26.   And I find *that what is* more bitter than death *itself, is* the woman, whose heart *is but* snares and nets, *and* her hands *are as* bands *of captivity.* Whoso *shall desire to* pleaseth God shall *endeavor to* escape

from her. But the sinner shall *blindly* be taken by her.

27.　　Behold, this have I found *to be true*, saith the preacher, *accurately* **counting** one by one, to find out the *full* account,

28.　　Which yet my soul seeketh *for*, but I find not. One man *who is faithful* among a thousand have I found. But a *faithful* woman among all those, have I not found.

29.　　Lo, this only have I found *out*, that God hath made man upright *at the beginning*. But they have sought out many inventions *with which to sin and to transgress against the Lord*.

CHAPTER 8

1.　　Who *is living* as the wise *man*? And who knoweth the *understanding and* interpretation of a thing? A man's *natural* wisdom maketh his face to shine, and the boldness of his face shall be changed *because of it*.

2.　　I *counsel thee* to keep the kings's commandment, and *also* **that**, in regard*s* of the oath of God.

3.　　Be not hasty to go out of his sight. Stand not *before him* in an evil thing. For he doeth whatsoever *it is that* pleaseth him.

4.   Where the word of a king *is, there is* power. And who may say unto him, What doest thou?

5.   Whoso keepeth the commandment *of the Lord* shall feel no evil thing. And a wise man's heart discerneth both *the* time and *the reason for* judgment.

6.   Because to every purpose there is *a specified* time and *a decreed* judgment, therefore the misery of *any* man *is* great*ly* upon him.

7.   For he knoweth not, that which shall be *in the days ahead.* For who can tell *unto* him when it shall be?

8.   *There is* no man that hath power over the spirit *of his being,* to *be able to* retain the spirit *within him.* Neither *hath he any more* power in the day of *his* death. And *there is* no discharge *exercised within that* war. Neither shall wickedness deliver those that are given to it.

9.   All this have I seen *personally,* and applied my heart unto every work that is done under the sun. *There is* a time wherein one man ruleth over another *unto* his own hurt.

10.   And so I saw the wicked *ultimately* buried, who had come and gone from the place of the holy, and they were *completely* forgotten in the city where they had so done *their wickedness.* This *is* also *a* vanity.

11.   Because sentence against an evil work is not *usually* executed speedily, therefore the heart of the *wicked* sons of men, is fully set in them to do evil.

12.   Though a sinner do evil an hundred times, and *yet by grace* his *days* be prolonged, yet surely I know *from within* that it shall be well with them that fear God, which *walk in godly* fear before him.

13.   But it shall not be well with the wicked, neither shall he prolong *his* days *of himself,* **which are** as a shadow. Because he *chooseth to* feareth not before God.

14.   There is a vanity which is done upon the earth: that there be just *men*, unto whom it happeneth *unto them, just like* according to the work of the wicked. Again, there be wicked *men*, to whom it happeneth *unto them, just like* according to the work of the righteous. I said that this also *is a* vanity.

15.   Then I commended *the joy of* mirth, because a man hath no better thing under the sun, than to eat, and to drink, and to be merry. For that *mirth* shall abide with him *as a result* of his labour, *all of* the days of his life, which God giveth *unto* him under the sun.

16.   When I applied mine heart to know *natural* wisdom, and to see the business that is done upon

the earth: (for also *there is that*, *which* neither day nor night seeth sleep with his eyes),

17.   Then I beheld all *of* the work of God, that a man cannot find out *all of* the work that is done under the sun. Because though a man labour to seek *it* out, yet he shall not find *it*. Yea farther, though a wise *man* think to know *it*, yet shall he not be able to find *it*.

CHAPTER 9

1.   For all this, I considered in my heart even to declare all this, that the righteous, and the wise, and their works, *are* in the hand of God. No man knoweth either *the* love or *the* hatred *by* all *that is* before them.

2.   All *things* *concerning life's activities*, **come** alike *un*to all. *There is* one event *gendering un*to the right-eous, and *un*to *all* the wicked *as well*. To the good, and to the clean, and to the unclean *also*. To him that sacrificeth *unto the Lord*, and to him that sacri-ficeth not *unto the Lord*. As *it is gendered unto* the good, so *is it gendered unto* the sinner. *And to* he that sweareth, as *well as to* **he** that *reverently* feareth an oath.

3.   This *is* an evil among all *things* that are done under the sun, that *there is indeed* one event

unto all. Yea, also the heart of the sons of *sinful* men is full of evil, and madness *is* in their heart while they live, and after that, **they go** *into the Nether World,* **to** *join those who dwell among* the *spiritually* **dead.**

4.   For to him that is *currently* joined to all *of* the living, there is *still* hope *to surrender to Christ.* For a living dog is better *off* than a dead lion.

5.   For the living know *the reality* that they shall *physically* die, but the *spiritually and physically* dead *individuals that have gone on,* know not any thing *more of what is happening on the earth,* neither have they any more *promise of* a reward. For the memory of them is forgotten.

6.   Also their love, and their hatred, and their envy, is now perished *along with them.* Neither have they any more a *promised* portion for ever in any *thing* that is done under the sun.

7.   *So,* go thy way, eat thy bread with joy, and drink thy wine with a merry heart. For *today is the day of salvation, and* God now accepteth thy works.

8.   Let thy garments be always white *with righteousness,* and let thy head lack no ointment.

9.   Live joyfully with the wife *of thy youth,* whom thou lovest all the days of the life of thy vanity; which he hath given *unto* thee under the sun, all the days of thy vanity. For that *is* thy portion in

this life, and in thy labour which thou takest under the sun.

10.   Whatsoever thy hand findeth to do, do *it* with *all of* thy might. For *there is* no work, nor device, nor knowledge, nor wisdom, *with*in the grave, whither thou *art destined to* goest.

11.   I returned, and *I* saw under the sun, that the race *is* not to the swift, nor the battle to the strong, neither yet *is* bread *given* to the wise, nor yet riches to men of understanding, nor yet favour to men of skill. But time and chance happeneth *alike un*to them all.

12.   For *a* man also knoweth not his time *of departure*. As the fishes that are taken in an evil net, and as the birds that are caught in the snare, so *are* the sons of *sinful* men snared *by death* in an evil time, when it falleth suddenly upon them.

13.   This *natural* wisdom have I seen also under the sun, and it *seemed* great unto me.

14.   *There was* a little city, and few *sinful* men within it, and there came a great king against it, and besieged it, and built great bulwarks against it.

15.   Now there was found *with*in it a poor wise man, and he by his wisdom delivered the city. Yet no man remembered that same poor man.

16.   Then said I, *Natural* wisdom *is* better than *physical* strength. Nevertheless the poor man's *natural* wisdom *is* despised, and his words are not heard.

17.   The words of wise *men are* heard in quiet, more than the cry of him that ruleth among fools.

18.   *Natural* wisdom *is* better than weapons of war, but *sadly* one sinner destroyeth much good.

CHAPTER 10

1.   Dead flies cause the ointment of the apothecary to send forth a stinking savour. *So doth* a little folly *unto* him that is in reputation for wisdom *and* honour.

2.   A wise man's heart *is* at his right hand, but a fool's heart *is* at his left.

3.   Yea also, when he that is a fool walketh by the way, his wisdom faileth *him*, and *by his actions* he saith to every one *that* he *is* a fool.

4.   If the spirit of the ruler *of the people* rise up against thee, leave not thy *appointed* place; for yielding *to the ruler,* pacifieth great offences.

5.   There is an evil *which* I have seen under the sun, *it is* as an *grievous* error *which* proceedeth from the ruler.

6.   Folly is *promoted, and* set in great dignity, and the rich *are demoted, and* sit in low place.

7.	I have seen servants *riding* upon horses, and *the genuine* princes walking as servants upon the earth.

8.	He that diggeth a pit *to snare another,* shall *surely* fall into it *himself.* And whoso breaketh *down* an hedge, a *hidden* serpent shall bite him.

9.	Whoso removeth *the heavy* stones shall be hurt therewith. *And* he that cleaveth *the* wood *with a dull edge,* shall be endangered thereby.

10.	If the iron be blunt and he do not whet the edge, then must he put *forth, even* to *the* more strength. But wisdom *is* profitable to *give* direct*ion*.

11.	Surely the serpent will bite without *any* enchantment. And a babbler *of words* is no better.

12.	The words of a wise man's mouth *are* gracious. But the lips of a fool will *eventually* swallow up himself.

13.	The beginning of the words of his mouth *is proven to be* foolishness. And the end of his talk *is clearly seen as* mischievous madness.

14.	A fool also is *chock* full of words. A *natural sinful* man cannot tell what shall be. And *even* what shall be *coming* after him, who can *prevail upon, and* tell him?

15.	The labour of the foolish wearieth every one of them, because he knoweth not how to go *in*to the city.

16. Woe to thee, O land, when thy king *is* a child, and thy princes, *through intemperance,* eat in the morning!

17. Blessed *art* thou, O land, when thy king *is* the son of nobles, and thy princes eat *their fill* in due season, for *their* strength, and not for *their* drunkenness.

18. By much slothfulness the building decayeth *and falleth.* And through idleness of the hands the house droppeth through.

19. A feast is made for laughter and wine maketh merry, but money *is put forth to* answereth all *things.*

20. Curse not the king, no not in thy thought*s.* And curse not the rich in thy bedchamber. For a bird of the air shall carry the voice *of thy curse* and that which hath wings shall tell the matter *to another.*

CHAPTER 11

1. Cast thy bread upon the waters, for thou shalt find it after many days.

2. Give a portion to seven, and also to eight. For thou knowest not what evil shall be upon the earth.

3. If the clouds be full of rain, they empty *themselves* upon the earth. And if the tree fall*eth*

toward the south, or toward the north, *then* in the place where the tree falleth, there it shall be.

4.   He that observeth the wind, *and acts accordingly,* shall not sow. And he that regardeth the *condition of the* clouds shall not reap.

5.   As thou knowest not what *is* the way of the *Human* spirit, *nor* how the bones *do grow with*in the womb of her that is with child, even so thou knowest not the works of God who maketh all *things*.

6.   In the morning sow thy seed, and in the evening withhold not thine hand. For thou knowest not whether *it* shall prosper, either this *way* or that, or whether they both *shall be* alike good.

7.   Truly the light *is* sweet, and a pleasant *thing it is* for the eyes to behold the sun.

8.   But if a man live*s* many years, *and* rejoice*s* in them all, yet let him remember the days of darkness. For they shall be many. All that cometh, *whether bright days or dark days, it is a* vanity.

9.   Rejoice, O young man, in thy youth, and let thy heart cheer thee in the days of thy youth, and walk *fully* in the ways of thine heart, and in the sight of thine eyes. But know thou *this*, that for all *of* these *things* God will *surely* bring thee into judgment.

10. Therefore remove sorrow from thy heart, and put away *the* evil from thy flesh. For childhood and youth are *a once experienced* vanity.

CHAPTER 12

1. Remember *even* now thy Creator, *while* in the days of thy youth, while the evil days *that are yet ahead* come not, nor *yet* the years *of future despair* draw nigh, when thou shalt *surely* say, I have no pleasure in them.

2. While the sun, or the light *of day*, or the moon, or the stars, be not darkened, nor *even* the clouds return*ing* after the rain.

3. In the day when the keepers of the house shall tremble *before the Lord God*, and the strong men shall bow themselves, and the grinders *shall* cease because they are few, and those that look out of the windows *that are to* be darkened,

4. And the doors shall be shut *that lead* in*to* the streets, when the sound of the grinding is *brought* low, and he shall rise up *early* at the voice of the bird, and all *of* the daughters of musick shall be brought low.

5. Also *when* they shall be afraid of *that which is* high *and exalted*, and *many* fears *shall be* in the way, and the almond tree shall flourish *and grow*,

and the grasshopper shall be a burden, and *the* desire *of the heart* shall fail. Because *sinful* man goeth to his long *awaited* home *of death*, and the mourners go about the streets *in vain*.

6.   Or ever the silver cord *shall* be loosed, or the golden bowl *shall* be broken, or the pitcher *for the water shall* be broken at the fountain, or the *labouring* wheel *shall be* broken at the cistern.

7.   Then shall the *body made of* dust return to the earth as it was. And the *Human* spirit *of the redeemed* shall return unto God who *originally* gave it.

8.   Vanity of vanities, saith the preacher; all *is* vanity.

9.   And moreover, because the preacher was *naturally* wise, he still taught the people knowledge. Yea, he gave good heed *unto*, and sought out *diligently*, *and* set in order many proverbs.

10.   The preacher sought to find out acceptable words. And *that which was* written *within the Scriptures was* upright, *even* words of truth.

11.   The words of the wise *are* as goads, and as nails fastened *by* the *building* masters of assemblies, *which* are given from one shepherd.

12.   And further, by these, my son, be admonished. Of making many books *there is* no end. And much study *of natural things is* a weariness of the flesh.

13.   Let us hear the conclusion of the whole matter: Fear *the living* God, and keep his *Royal Law* commandments. For this *is* the whole *duty* of man.

14.   For God shall bring every work *of man* into judgment, with every secret thing *being revealed*, whether *it be* good, or whether *it be* evil.

Epilogue

With the reading of the Book of Ecclesiastes, the futility of life, apart from God, becomes increasingly clear.

Because the driving force of sin will compel men to do what they say they do not want to do, and visa-versa, for one to find themselves here on this Earth, and then not know why they are here is, to say the least, frustrating.

God specifically designed human men and women to ultimately become his very own family members. This only becomes possible through the finished work of Jesus Christ of Nazareth, upon the cross of Calvary.

A New-Birth of the Human spirit will catapult an individual into a realm that is not spoken of as often as it should be, in an intelligent manner. That realm of newness is designed to have an effect upon every area of a person's life.

With a new spiritual birth a Human-Being becomes supernatural, and with the help of the Holy Spirit of God, able to conquer any obstacle that would present itself.

Solomon experienced the vanity of natural day-to-day existence. And he knew that the natural was not all that God desired for men. Choose the spiritual, and prepare for an out-of-this-world future.

Maranantha!

Meet the Author

By-The-Book Ministries, Inc. began in 2001 as a teaching outreach. Rob E. Daley has been gifted by God to be able to explain biblical truths in an easy to understand manner.

Many have been blessed by his teaching style.

Rob was saved and filled with the Holy Spirit in 1978 and has been instructed by the greatest teacher of all—the Spirit of Truth Himself. Rob is an ordained minister with the Assemblies of God International Fellowship and has pastored in various churches over the past 34 years.

It is the desire of this ministry to see the body of Christ solidly taught, and grow up into the things of the Lord. Rob is available for seminars, retreats, conventions, etc.

Rob can be reached at:

thedaleys@bythebookministries.org

http://robdaleyauthor.com

.

www.ingramcontent.com/pod-product-compliance
Lightning Source LLC
Chambersburg PA
CBHW020953030426
42339CB00004B/88